Our Favorites

Graphing

Suzanne Barchers

Publishing Credits

Dona Herweck Rice, *Editor-in-Chief*; Lee Aucoin, *Creative Director*; Don Tran, *Print Production Manager*; Sara Johnson, *Senior Editor*; Jamey Acosta, *Assistant Editor*; Neri Garcia, *Interior Layout Designer*; Stephanie Reid, *Photo Editor*; Rachelle Cracchiolo, M.A.Ed., *Publisher*

Image Credits

Teacher Created Materials

5301 Oceanus Drive
Huntington Beach, CA 92649-1030
http://www.tcmpub.com

ISBN 978-1-4333-0430-9

©2011 Teacher Created Materials, Inc.
Printed in China

Table of Contents

Looking Back

It is the last week of school. Our class talks about what we like best.

We will make a book of favorites for next year's class.

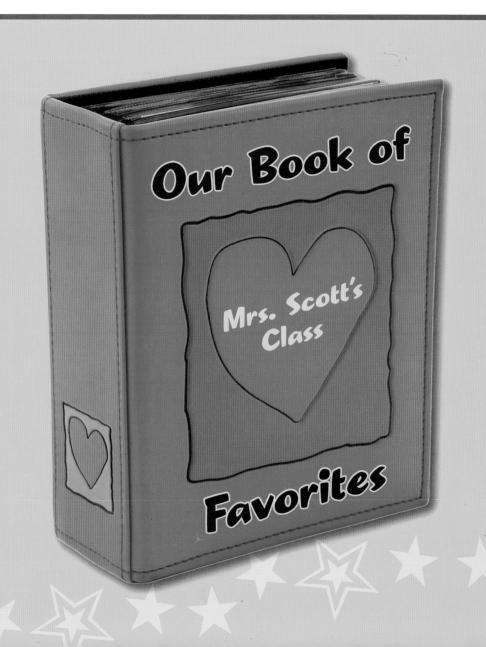

Our Favorites

We start with our favorite lunch.
We make a list of the 4 top lunches.
Then we vote.

Our Favorite Lunch	
fish sticks	|||
spaghetti	|||||	
chicken nuggets	||||| ||
pizza	||||| ||||

No one is surprised by the winning lunch.

Our Favorite Lunch

a. Which lunch was the most favorite?

b. Which lunch was the least favorite?

c. How many more people voted for pizza than chicken nuggets?

Our class has 4 kinds of pets. We have 10 fish in an **aquarium**. There are 2 mice that live in a cage.

The information we collect is called **data**.

We have 1 hamster. We have 3 frogs.
We make a **graph** of our favorite
class pets.

Our Favorite Class Pets

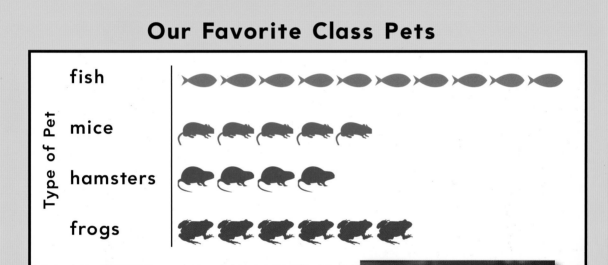

This is a **pictograph**.
This type of graph uses
pictures and symbols
to show data.

We like to read a lot. We can not choose just one kind of book.

We make a list of our favorite kinds of books. Then we vote.

Our Favorite Kinds of Books	
fantasy	||||
nonfiction	~~||||~~ |||
adventure	||||
poetry	|||
comics	~~||||~~ |

We make a graph to show our favorites.

You can look at the graph to see
our favorites.

Our Favorite Books

We all like to play sports. We vote on soccer, softball, jump rope, and kickball.

We make a graph of our votes to put in the book.

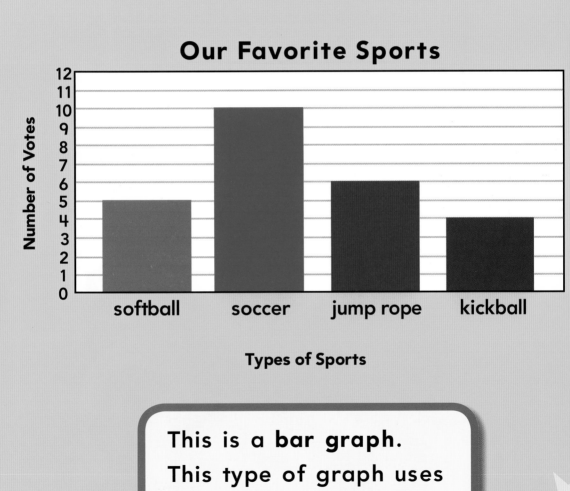

Our Favorite Sports

Number of Votes

| | softball | soccer | jump rope | kickball |

Types of Sports

This is a **bar graph**. This type of graph uses bars to show data.

We make a list of school subjects.
We vote on our favorite ones.

Our Favorite School Subjects	
math	6
reading	6
social studies	5
science	4
writing	4

It is hard to choose a favorite.
The votes are very close.

LET'S EXPLORE MATH

Look at the bar graph. Answer the questions.

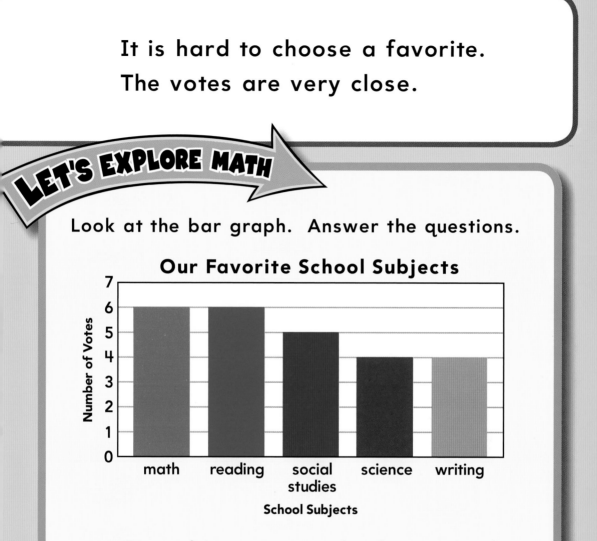

Our Favorite School Subjects

a. Two subjects are equal. They are tied for the most favorite. What are they?

b. Two other subjects are equal. They are tied for the least favorite. What are they?

c. How many more people voted for math than voted for science?

We think about the **field trips** we went on this year. We make a list of the trips.

We vote on our favorite field trip by raising our hands.

Our Favorite Field Trips	
zoo	卌 |||
aquarium	卌	
park	||
museum	|||
theater	卌

We make a bar graph to put in the book.

LET'S EXPLORE MATH

Look at the bar graph. Answer the questions.

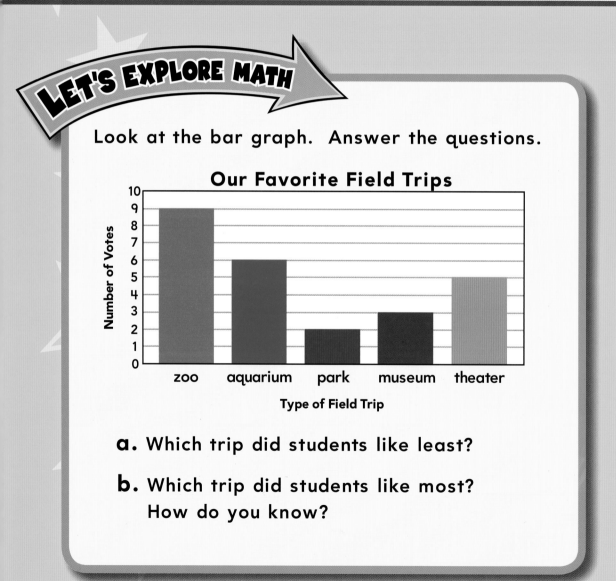

a. Which trip did students like least?

b. Which trip did students like most?
   How do you know?

We make a list of our favorite school days.

Our Favorite Days
Field Day
100th Day
Valentine's Day

We liked Valentine's Day best. We liked making cards in art class.

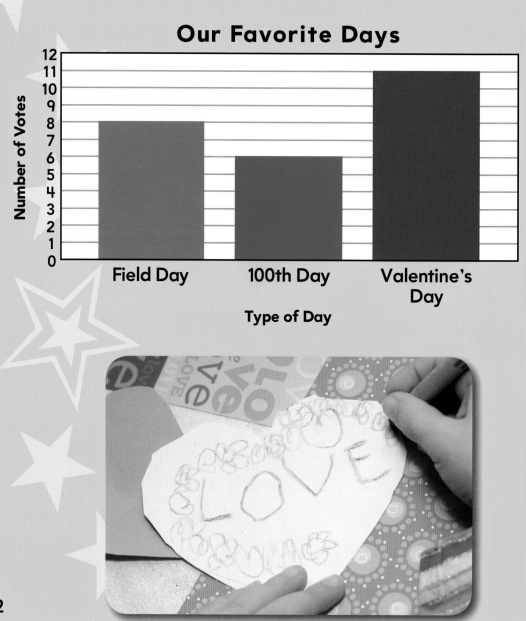

Our Favorite Days

Number of Votes

12
11
10
9
8
7
6
5
4
3
2
1
0

Field Day   100th Day   Valentine's Day

Type of Day

We took the cards to a nursing home.

Happy Valentine's Day!

We make a list of our favorite snacks. Then we vote for our favorite one.

Our Favorite Snacks	
snack	vote
popcorn	9
crackers	4
apples	5
oranges	7
pretzels	0

We make a graph of our favorites.
We get to have the winning snack on
the last day of school!

Look at the pictograph. Answer the questions.

Our Favorite Snacks

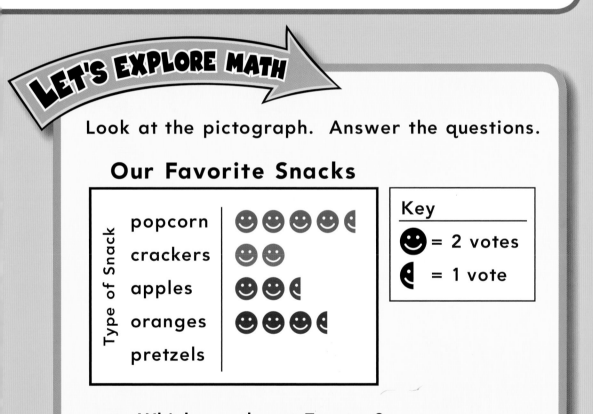

a. Which snack got 7 votes?

b. Which snack got no votes?

c. Which snack does the class get on the
   last day of school?

25

The Last Day

Our class surprises Mrs. Scott on the last day of school. We have made a big graph.

Favorite Teacher

Then we all eat lots of popcorn and read our book.

Favorite Pets

Mr. Lee's class is gathering data about everyone's favorite pets. Each person in the class votes for his or her favorite pet. The votes are shown in the tally chart below. Make a bar graph using this data. Then answer the questions below.

Favorite Pets	
dog	𝍫𝍫 𝍦𝍦
cat	𝍫𝍫 𝍦𝍦𝍦
bird	𝍫𝍫 𝍦
hamster	𝍦𝍦𝍦𝍦
turtle	𝍦𝍦

a. Which pet is liked most?

b. Which pet is liked least?

c. How many more people like birds than turtles?

28

Solve It!

Use the steps below to help you solve the problem.

Step 1: Copy this bar graph.

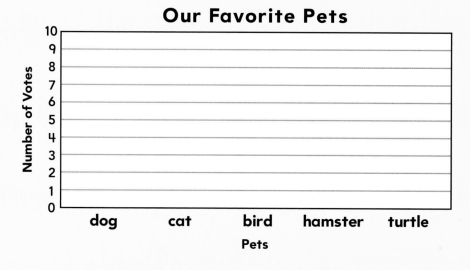

Step 2: Look at the tally chart. How many people like cats? Make a bar that shows that number of people.

Step 3: Look at the tally chart. How many people like dogs? Make a bar that shows that number of people.

Step 4: Finish the bar graph for the other animals. Then answer the questions.

Glossary

aquarium—a place to go and look at water animals; tank of water where fish are kept

bar graph—a graph that uses bars to show information

data—a collection of information

field trip—a visit to a special place, such as a park or a zoo

graph—a diagram that shows information and how it is related

nursing home—a place where older or sick people live

pictograph—a graph that uses pictures to show information

Index

Let's Explore Math

Page 7:
a. pizza
b. fish sticks
c. 2 more people

Page 17:
a. math and reading
b. science and writing
c. 2 more people

Page 20:
a. the park
b. the zoo; it has the most votes

Page 25:
a. oranges
b. pretzels
c. popcorn

Solve the Problem

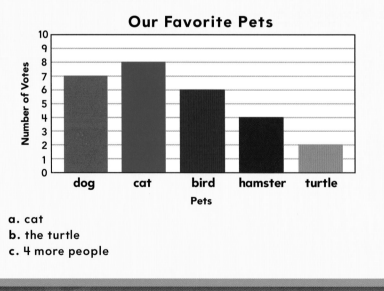

Our Favorite Pets

a. cat
b. the turtle
c. 4 more people